W9-AVT-097

FUNERALS
WITHOUT GOD

FUNERALS WITHOUT GOD

A Practical Guide to Non-Religious Funerals

by Jane Wynne Willson

Prometheus Books

59 John Glenn Drive
Amherst, New York 14228-2119

There is a growing need for help with non-religious ceremonies, as our society increasingly abandons religion and adopts a non-theistic life stance. This booklet seeks, in a totally practical way, to help those who want to organize a non-religious funeral ceremony for the first time.

This book has been written and compiled by Jane Wynne Willson. She acknowledges with gratitude the help of the following, who contributed encouragement, material, ideas, and constructive criticism: Bill Brown, Maeve Denby, Sue Lines, C. D. Miller, Joan Knowles, George Brown, Maeve Mepham, Brian Nicol, Richard Paterson, Diana Rookledge, Allan Shell, Barbara Smoker, Harry Stopes-Roe, Nicolas Walter, Robin Wood, and members of her own family.

She thanks the executors of the estate of C. Day Lewis and also Jonathan Cape and Hogarth Press for permission to reprint "A Time to Dance"; and Richard Scott Simon Ltd. for permission to include the poem by Joyce Grenfell.

Published 1990 by Prometheus Books

Funerals without God: A Practical Guide to Non-Religious Funerals. Copyright © 1990 by British Humanist Association. All rights reserved. No part of this publication may be reproduced, stored in a retrieval system, or transmitted in any form or by any means, electronic, mechanical, photocopying, recording, or otherwise, without prior written permission of the publisher, except in the case of brief quotations embodied in critical articles and reviews.

Inquiries should be addressed to
Prometheus Books, 59 John Glenn Drive, Amherst, New York 14228-2119.
VOICE: 716–691–0133, ext. 210.
FAX: 716–691-0137.
WWW.PROMETHEUSBOOKS.COM

09   12 11 10 9 8

Library of Congress Catalog Number: 90-063185
ISBN 13: 978-0-87975-641-3
ISBN 10: 0-87975-641-1

Printed in the United States of America   CIP

Printed in the United States of America on acid-free paper

CONTENTS

 # INTRODUCTION

THE NEED FOR CEREMONY

We know that throughout history, and indeed pre-history, ceremonies have been used to mark important events in people's lives, and a formal occasion can be particularly helpful in the early days of bereavement. The public expression and sharing of grief are generally considered an essential part of recovery after the death of someone close, and the opportunity for this shared grieving is provided by the various world religions according to their own rites. But it can be both distasteful and distressing for those present if a religious service is carried out for someone who had no religious belief.

While it is possible to instruct a funeral director to organize a completely private cremation, this will give none of the mutual support that a ceremony can provide. So the various Humanist and secularist organizations have been in demand to help with non-religious ceremonies for well over a century, either by providing an officiant or by giving advice and help to families and friends who wish to carry out such a ceremony themselves. We use the word 'ceremony' rather than 'service', as we see it as an occasion to celebrate a human life that has ended and to provide mutual support and comfort for the living, rather than as a 'service' to God.

THE GROWTH IN DEMAND

In our increasingly secular society, where for example more than half of all weddings no longer take place in church, the demand for non-religious funerals is ever on the increase. This has presented the Humanist movement with a considerable problem. Our ceremonies are by their very nature personal celebrations of an individual's life. To commercialize and standardize these ceremonies would be to destroy those very features that make them so sensitive, so genuine and so much appreciated. Yet, as the demand for officiants grows, we are finding it increasingly difficult to meet the need in all parts of the country.

THE AIM OF THIS BOOKLET

The main purpose of this booklet is twofold: to help Humanists who are thinking of becoming officiants on a regular basis; and to help families and friends who are faced with the need to organize a ceremony themselves at short notice. A third group who may find parts of it useful are funeral directors coping with funerals where there is no officiant and the family has no wish to play an active role.

The booklet aims to set out clearly the basic format of a Humanist ceremony, to suggest possible readings and turns of phrase, and to state simply the various practical measures that need to be taken. In short we have tried to put together a straightforward working manual.

We do not lay down rules about how such funeral ceremonies should be conducted. Each one will be tailored to suit the taste and wishes of the family and friends who will be there and the personality of the person who has died. Officiants too vary in their style and their choice of language. Words that sound flowery or archaic to one officiant, trip naturally from the tongue of another and sound perfectly appropriate. As they gain in experience and confidence, officiants will discover for themselves what suits them and how best they can manage. But most of us have found that clear guidelines and sample ceremonies on which to base our first attempts can be a considerable help.

2 SHALL WE DO IT OURSELVES?

THE CHOICES

On rare occasions a person who is expecting to die soon takes steps to arrange their own funeral, even discussing it with the friend or relative they would like to conduct it. Or they may get in touch with a Humanist officiant, to go over the kind of ceremony they would like to have. More usually the choice is made by others immediately after a death, when the ceremony is imminent. Once those responsible, usually the next of kin, have decided that a non-religious ceremony is appropriate, they should seriously consider whether they might prefer to organize a ceremony themselves, rather than seeking help from an outside agency.

This can be done. There are no rules and regulations which lay down that funerals must be conducted by registered officiants, or in a particular format, as is the case with weddings. In many ways a funeral ceremony conducted by a relative or friend can be the most satisfactory solution; on occasion it is the only option. To take an extreme example, when a death occurs in a very remote place—such as high on a Himalayan mountainside—the companions of the dead climber will stand round the makeshift grave and one of them will speak a few solemn words of farewell, before leaving the body of their friend. They have no choice in the matter.

In circumstances rather less extreme than the climber's death there may be no Humanist officiant conveniently available. Even when this is not the case there will often be a friend or relative who could do the job as well, or better than a stranger could hope to.

THE LAST TASK

Death from illness or old age often comes at the end of a long period of being cared for. Where this caring has been carried out by family or friends, who have attended to the sick person's needs and supported them up to the time of their death, there is in a sense just one task that remains—to give them a dignified funeral. There is an intimacy about a ceremony that is organized by those immediately involved, which cannot be achieved when it is conducted by an outsider. It seems the natural thing to do—the last service to someone for whom you have cared.

SHARING THE RESPONSIBILITY

Sometimes there is an obvious person to conduct the ceremony, who is prepared to take on the job. A certain amount of confidence is needed and no pressure should ever be exerted. It would be quite unreasonable to expect someone devastated by the death to take part in conducting the ceremony, or indeed anyone likely to be over emotional about it. Equally for someone painfully shy it might be too much of an ordeal. A good solution can be for two, or even three, people to share the responsibility—it is a great support not to be on one's own up in front.

TAKING THE PLUNGE

Once the family have decided to do the ceremony themselves, with or without help from friends, this booklet will show what has to be done and how to do it. The person or persons who will actually conduct the ceremony will be well advised to follow the suggestions step by step. Keep to the order given so far as possible, and compose the ceremony itself under the five headings listed, and you will find it all perfectly straightforward. Remember that your only responsibility is the formal part of the ceremony, since the overall management of the funeral is the job of the funeral director.

HOW ELABORATE NEED THE CEREMONY BE?

There is absolutely no need for the ceremony to he elaborate: it all depends on what seems appropriate for the particular individual and for the particular circumstances. Some families particularly request an extremely short and simple ceremony. Their concern to keep the occasion brief must of course be respected, but it should be borne in mind that it can seem rather abrupt to have a ceremony that is too short—literally a hail and Farewell, when the mourners go out almost as soon as they have come in. Five or six minutes is perhaps the minimum time for a meaningful and dignified ceremony.

In contrast, where the person has been well known in public life—in whatever sphere, either in their own locality or nationally—there will be much to say in the tribute. The general remarks can then be curtailed, and tributes, probably from several people, can be included. In these circumstances it may be appropriate to book a double session at the crematorium.

You will see that the first of the three sample ceremonies in this book is much the shortest. This was because the parents did not want poetry readings and passages from literature that would be foreign to their son's tastes and character. Quite often the bereaved family or friends feel they want to keep the ceremony short and simple—and of course their wishes must be respected. But it is reasonable to point out that a ceremony that is abruptly short may appear undignified, and can be less than satisfying to those present.

BEFORE THE CEREMONY

A certain amount of this chapter (the first two sections in particular) is written primarily for regular officiants, who are likely to be conducting the ceremony for someone they have never met. The points made do not in general apply to people organizing a ceremony within their own family or circle, where the deceased person is well known to them. However, some of the advice given in the chapter, and in particular the checklist of facts you need to know, could help to focus the thoughts even of the family officiant.

TAKING IT ON

If you are an established officiant you are most likely to be asked to conduct a non-religious funeral by a local funeral director, although sometimes the request may come from a friend or relative of the person who has died, from a local Humanist group or the Council for Democratic and Secular Humanism (CODESH). You will need to find out the following information at once:

- the time and place proposed for the funeral (if this has already been fixed) and the normal time allotted for each service at the crematorium (this is twenty minutes in most urban crematoria);

- the name, address and phone number of the relative or friend who is responsible for the funeral arrangements, and also of the funeral director;
- the circumstances and date of the death and any particular family circumstances that may already have been established. Every scrap of information you manage to pick up at this stage will make your visit to the family or friends that much easier;
- whether the deceased was a major figure, either locally or nationally, or a keen musician. If a double session needs to he booked at the crematorium, to allow time for a number of tributes or for a lot of music, this must be seen to at once by the funeral director.

Visiting the Family or Friends

Once you have agreed to take the ceremony, the most urgent thing to do is to arrange to visit the family or friends. The urgency lies in the fact that you probably have only a few days—at most a week—before the funeral, and you don't want to have to write the ceremony at the last minute. There are occasions when time, distance or some other factor makes a personal visit impossible. If that is the case a long telephone call—or several—will have to do. But it should be emphasized that a personal visit is much more satisfactory. It is a great comfort for the family to have met the person who will be 'up front' on the day, and it is an advantage for you to recognize the chief mourners when they arrive. But there is a more important reason for a personal visit. If you want to get a feel of what the deceased person was like, in order to present an accurate and sensitive picture of them at the ceremony, then you are more likely to succeed after visiting their home. Sometimes too there are several members of the family or friends present, who contribute anecdotes, suggest poems or music, and so on. It is always helpful if the family can show you a photograph.

You will get more out of your visit if you have forewarned the family about the sort of help you would be looking for—such as anecdotes to illustrate what the deceased person was like, ideas for music or poetry etc.

It will become evident early on in the visit if the ceremony is likely to be an elaborate or long one. Indeed the matter may already have been discussed with the funeral director when the cremation was arranged. It is perfectly possible, as was mentioned above, to book the crematorium for two or even three consecutive sessions for an extra charge, if it is available. In the case of someone for whom music was particularly important, for example, a short recital by professional musicians may already have been suggested.

During this visit it is important to run through the basic structure of the ceremony and the exact order of events. You should tell the family whether you will be at the entrance to the chapel to greet the chief mourners when they arrive, or if you prefer to be standing at the lectern. It is also a good idea to know if they wish to have the coffin carried into the crematorium (a) before any of the mourners enter the chapel (as is often the case if the family has a Jewish background); or (b) ahead of the chief mourners, in procession; or (c) after everyone is seated.

HOW HUMANIST SHOULD THE CEREMONY BE?

As well as the officiant finding out information from the relatives or friends of the person who has died, they in their turn will want to get some idea of the sort of ceremony that is taking shape in your mind. They may need reassurance that nothing will be said that could possibly offend anyone present who is religious. You can point out that there will be a short silence during the ceremony for people to think their own thoughts, when anyone wishing to pray silently will have the opportunity to do so. For someone who was all active Humanist, or whose beliefs and inclinations were positively Humanist, it is perfectly right and proper to include references to Humanism in the ceremony. This should be no more upsetting to someone present who has religious beliefs than a traditional religious funeral service would be to a Humanist, attending the funeral of a religious friend.

THE IMPORTANCE OF ACCURACY

It is a good idea to get impressions from more than the source, to avoid getting a one-sided picture of your subject. It is possible to ask for the phone number of a friend or relative whom you can have a further talk with. Although you certainly are not in the business of looking for skeletons in cupboards—and some family secrets are best left undiscovered—yet you do want to paint a picture that will be recognizable to all those present. Remember that, in the grief and remorse of bereavement, virtues are remembered and exaggerated, while human failings, that could be referred to without unkindness, are sometimes forgotten.

Make careful notes while you are there. It is crucial that the information you gather should be factually accurate. Try to note down actual words and phrases that people spontaneously use, as these can be very revealing and are often worth quoting. If you are able to write shorthand this is an enormous asset; alternatively, if you ask tactfully and explain the reason, there might be situations in which you could record an interview. Find out, if you can, the following:

(1)   the name by which s/he was usually known, as well as the full name;
(2)   an outline biography, including such things as childhood, education, work, places s/he lived, marriage or partnership, family, interests and hobbies;
(3)   any anecdotes you call glean—amusing, touching, characteristic;
(4)   the extent to which the deceased was a humanist or merely non-religious, and the history behind these beliefs;
(5)   his/her taste in music and books, or whether the family have any preferences or suggestions, so that appropriate choices can be made for using at the ceremony.

INVOLVING OTHERS

It is always valuable for others to be involved in conducting the ceremony, if they personally wish it. Sometimes you will find there is a family friend, relative or colleague who is glad to do some or all of the tribute. As this tends to be the central part of the ceremony, a personal tribute is a great asset. Obviously a friend or relative who knew the person well is likely to speak with greater authenticity than an outsider can ever hope to. It also saves the officiant some of the preparation. However in the majority of situations it is not possible, as those intimately involved feel they might show their emotions too much. In any case, the officiant should always be prepared to take over if necessary.

More often a member of the family will write a tribute which the officiant can read, or draw upon. Sometimes letters of condolence have already come which express well some aspect of the personality or character. Perhaps the recipient will let you read an extract from these at the funeral. Occasionally, a friend or relative volunteers to read a passage of prose or a poem, to play some music, or sing.

Perhaps it should just be mentioned a that, now and again, a member of the family or a friend may ask you to include a prayer or a hymn, or a religious reading. This is difficult, and officiants will vary as to how they tackle the situation. You could make it clear that, while you yourself cannot include something specifically religious, if someone wishes to contribute something on a personal basis, then you would be prepared to accept that, so long as no general act of worship resulted. Or you might prefer to dissuade them.

FURTHER CONTACT

Before leaving the family, suggest that they phone you if they have any further thoughts, anecdotes they would like you to refer to, or concerns. Reassure them that you will get to the crematorium in good time and that you will have arranged with the funeral director and the crematorium staff about the music that they have chosen, unless they have taken responsibility for this themselves.

THE CREMATORIUM

The vast majority of these ceremonies will take place at a crematorium. Now and again you may be asked to take a burial at a municipal cemetery, but this is rare. A number of the points in this section will apply to burials too.

Every crematorium is slightly different from others, but all will have certain features in common. The more familiar you are with these features, the easier will be your task on the day. Ideally you will have visited the building beforehand. In any event you will have to be in touch with the crematorium at some stage to let the organist know—if there is one—whether you want tapes or organ music. It is also useful to find out if there is a service immediately before yours. The funeral director will give you the telephone number of the crematorium.

If you are not familiar with the building it is wise to get there early to allow time for the staff to show you the layout of the building, the exits and entrances, the arrangements for music and the controls for removing or curtaining off the coffin at the committal.

The features that are common to almost all crematoria are the following:

(1) The chapel will be laid out like a small church, with pews in two main blocks and a section at the front that may be slightly raised.

(2) There will be one or sometimes two lecterns in that section. These are sometimes arranged at an angle so that you would be half turned towards the catafalque. In that case, if you prefer to face the assembled company, it may be possible to rearrange the lectern you are using.

(3) Within easy reach of the lectern will be one or more buttons. If there are several they will be clearly labeled. There is usually a button marked 'committal' which controls the removal or curtaining off of the coffin. In some crematoria, however, this is not under the control of the officiant but that of the organist or chapel attendant behind the scenes. There is often another button for you to indicate to the chapel attendant when the ceremony is over and the exit doors can be opened. Occasionally there is a button which controls the cassette player, but much more often this is done 'off stage'.

(4) There may be a cross and candles up in front and also prayer/hymn books set out on the pews. These are inappropriate for Humanist ceremonies, as indeed they are out of place for many other funerals. Crematoria are public buildings and do not belong to churches, so we have a right to ask that the cross he removed by the staff before the ceremony starts. The removal of the books is more difficult, as there may not be time for their reinstatement before the next funeral.

(5) There may be several doors. The main entrance will be where the coffin and the mourners come in. So as to avoid the people arriving for the next service coming face to face with those leaving the chapel, the exit is often different and usually to one side of the building, though special arrangements may have to be made for wheelchairs. One of your duties as officiant will be to lead the chief mourners out by the correct doors when the ceremony is over.

(6) The catafalque on which the coffin rests during the ceremony will be on the platform either to the side or behind where you are standing at the lectern.

(7) As well as an organist (whose services you may or may not be seeking) there will be one or two crematorium staff who are there to help.

(8)   There is usually a vestry which you can use as your base before the ceremony.

The Funeral Director

Your contact with the funeral director is likely to have started early on in the proceedings. If it has not, you should telephone the firm forthwith to let them know that you are going to act as officiant. It is their responsibility to see that the funeral arrangements run smoothly, so they are always helpful and supportive.

Discuss with the funeral director all the practical details and the precise timing of the whole operation. The matter of the fee is likely to be raised, so this is the time to let him know—if you are a regular officiant—what you will be charging and also any additional expenses you may have incurred. He will act as intermediary between you and whoever is paying the funeral expenses, and will generally hand you an envelope containing the fee just before the funeral. When the ceremony is being conducted by a member of the family or by a friend, payment will obviously not arise. (If you are unsure about current charges, advice call be sought from CODESH. There is sometimes a reduced charge for members of a Humanist organization. It is your responsibility to decide, and inform the funeral director, if in any particular case you feel that the fee should be reduced or waived.)

4 COMPOSING THE CEREMONY

You have now collected all the information you need about your subject, and your next task is to gather it together into a ceremony that will be as appropriate as you can make it. This is quite a challenge. But once it is wrapped up and ready you will feel able to sit back and relax.

PREPARING THE TEXT

Even if you are a sufficiently experienced public speaker to deliver some of it from notes or off the cuff, it is as well to have the text written out. There are a number of reasons for this. It gives you a feeling of confidence to have it there; copies can be given to anyone else who is taking part (such as someone giving the tribute, or the person organizing taped music), with their cues marked in; quite often one is asked for a copy of the ceremony afterwards; also, should the worst occur and you go down with laryngitis at the last moment, someone else could step in and read it. But perhaps the most important reason of all for writing it out is that you can then try it through for length. The timing is very important; if someone else is involved in the tribute or if, for some particular reason, there is extra music incorporated in the ceremony, it is crucial that no single part should overrun its time. You must be clear of the building in time for the staff to prepare for the next service.

THE STRUCTURE OF THE CEREMONY

To aid clarity we have divided the ceremony into the following separate sections:

A. Opening Words   D. The Committal
B. Thoughts on Life and Death   E. Closing Words
C. The Tribute

These sections are for convenience; also the suggestions for texts and turns of phrase are more easily listed under these headings. But there is no need whatever to keep to them rigidly, nor indeed to include all the sections. Some officiants prefer to launch straight into Section B, without any personal words of introduction. Sections B and C (Thoughts on Life and Death and the Tribute) can and often do merge with each other, and the length of each will depend largely on how much it is possible to say about the person's life. On occasion, so little can be discovered that, general remarks padded out with some suitable readings have to form the core of the ceremony,

A. Opening Words

These are words of welcome. You must remember that most, if not all, the people present will have little idea what a Humanist funeral ceremony is like. They need reassurance. You may wish to explain why a simple, non-religious ceremony is particularly fitting for the occasion; and how all human beings share concern when somebody has died.

B. Thoughts on Life and Death

This section can be built up with readings, both of poetry and prose, which in your judgment best reflect the circumstances of this particular person's life and death. Now and again the family will have suggested a favorite poem or author; more often you will have to make your own choices, guided by the information you have picked up. Readings and thoughts that would be suitable for a young man with a life of promise before him, killed in an accident, would obviously not be the same as those you would choose for a very old person, who has faded peacefully away at the end of a long and fulfilling life. By using extracts from great literature, this part of the ceremony can add dignity to the occasion. Further, without wishing to wallow in emotion, poetry, like music, can soothe and release pent-up feelings in some people which will help in the long process of grieving.

C. *The Tribute*

This, as has been said, is the core of the ceremony. It is the part where we celebrate the life that has ended, where good qualities and fine characteristics can be extolled, though the portrait painted must be a recognizable portrayal of the person concerned, mentioning human failings too, as appropriate. Anecdotes and stories to illustrate the person's life, some amusing if possible, can be remembered and told. Where the information you have gleaned is scant—and this can happen—your best course is to expand the general comments and the readings in Section B and merely give the bare biographical facts that you have available when you reach the tribute. The same is necessary on the rare occasions when the relatives are quite unable to come up with any pleasant memories at all, because there was no love lost between them, or because their dead relative was clearly a bad-tempered, selfish, cruel or thoroughly unpleasant individual.

But, as has been mentioned, if you are able to get impressions from more than one source, this can sometimes yield a totally different picture of the individual.

D. *The Committal*

The actual words at the moment of committal must be formal and brief, as this is the most stressful stage of the ceremony. The removal or curtaining off of the coffin can start either during or after these words. Music can be helpful.

You may sometimes be asked by the family to have no committal at all, to avoid distress, but to leave the coffin in full view throughout the ceremony. This is not a good idea, as it can mean mourners being reluctant to leave at the end of the ceremony. More important still, it can be more distressing for them in the long run than the symbolic removal or curtaining off of the coffin. This can actually help the bereaved come to terms with the fact of death and its finality.

E. Closing Words

A few remarks to round off the ceremony are appropriate, and sometimes, on behalf of the family, it is nice to thank everyone for having come to share in the occasion (see third ceremony). Finally, on a positive and determined note, express the resolve that we should all return to our own lives, enriched and strengthened.

THE FINISHED ARTICLE

It may seem an unnecessary detail to mention the size of paper and of print that you use. However, if one is not accustomed to using a lectern, if one's eyesight is not first class, or if one is tall, this can present a problem. Lecterns are not in general very high, though there is some variation, and a large proportion of regular officiants are in the retired age bracket. Consequently they are likely to wear reading glasses with a strictly limited depth of vision. If this is the case it is wise to write or print the text in bold, large print.

There is generally room on the lectern for two plies of standard $8\frac{1}{2} \times 11$ paper. If you use one side of the paper only and push the sheet you have just finished to one side, this causes the least commotion—in fact what you are doing cannot be seen by the assembled company. Alternatively you can hold your papers. In any event it is important to speak clearly and moderately slowly, projecting your voice to reach those at the back. The commonest mistakes made by beginners are to speak too fast and keep their heads down. Officiants should be sufficiently familiar with their text to be able to look at their audience from time to time while talking, not obviously reading every word. Remember that pauses are both effective and helpful.

THREE SAMPLE CEREMONIES

The following pages contain the texts of three sample funeral ceremonies. These are adapted from three ceremonies that have been used in the past few years, the names have been altered, and a few details have been changed or omitted.

The idea of including full texts is to show how the careful selection of material, much of which can be found elsewhere in this book, can produce three very different ceremonies. The officiant in "each of these cases has gone to some lengths to compose a tribute that gives a sensitive and genuine portrait or their subject; it is only in the second of our three ceremonies that both the officiant and also the person who delivered the tribute were members of the family.

It will be noted that, where use has been made of turns of phrase and texts that are included in our list (in chapter 7), these are given in full. Where actual passages or poems are used, they are quoted in full in the sample ceremonies and are omitted from chapter 8 (Poetry and Prose Readings).

FIRST CEREMONY

This ceremony was held for a young man who took his own life.

Opening Words

We have come together today to honor the life of Richard Evans, to remember him and to make our farewells.

This is not a religious ceremony: that would not have been in accord with Dick's view of life. I am here to speak for the human community of which he was part.

Thoughts on Life and Death

Death is a very personal matter for those who know it in someone close to them. But we are all concerned, directly or indirectly, with the death of any individual, for we are all members of one human community, and no one of us is independent and separate. Though some of the links are strong and some are tenuous, each of us is joined to all others by links of kinship, love, friendship, by living in the same neighborhood or town or country, or simply by our own common humanity. No one who encountered Dick failed to be warmed by his zest for the adventures of life, and his capacity for affection and friendship. And no one who knows of his tragic death will remain untouched by it, nor fail to ask themselves if they could have done anything to prevent it.

No one should be afraid of death itself: it is as natural as life. Only Nature is permanent. All that has life has its beginning and end ... and life exists in the time span between birth and death. For those of us who do not have a religious faith, and who believe that death brings the end of individual existence, life's significance lies in the experiences and satisfactions we achieve in that span of time; its permanence lies in the memories of those who knew us, and any influence we have left behind. The delight and laughter which packed Dick's short life will live in the memories of his family and friends much longer than the bewilderment over the choice he made at the end. We should be daring enough to remember him with happiness.

Joyce Grenfell's poem speaks for us:

> 'If I should go before the rest of you,
> Break not a flower, nor inscribe it stone,
> Nor, when I'm gone, speak in a Sunday voice,
> But be the usual selves that I have known.
> Weep if you must:

> Parting is hell,
> But life goes on
> So...sing as well!'

The Tribute

Dick went to Park Royal School in Leicester and the friendships that started there and at his primary school lasted all his life. After school he followed chances and opportunities wherever they led, and traveled from place to place in England and on the Continent. It is typical of his talent for entering fully into the life of the group in which he found himself that he acquired a command of fluent conversational French, though he had learned none at school.

He had only to see a group of lads kicking a football around in a park to become an enthusiastic member of the game. He made friends everywhere and joined in every adventure that was going—and in all manner of pranks and jokes too. All the family snapshots of Dick show him happy and laughing—everybody knew his broad grin and his strokes of luck. Every summer was for him a lovely summer.

Dick fitted as much varied experience into his thirty years as most of us do into a long life. His links with his family were close and loving. Perhaps he realized that settling down, staying in one place, and possibly forming a permanent relationship, were not for him. The last months of his life saw him depressed and quite unlike himself. But let us remember Dick for his enthusiasm and enjoyment, and for the warmth and love that radiated from him.

The Committal

Will you please stand for the committal. Here, in this last act, immune now to the changes and chances of our mortal lot, we commit the body of Richard Evans to its natural end.

Closing Words

In sadness for his death but with appreciation for his life, we remember Dick and his talent for joy and love. Finally, as we leave to continue our own voyage of discovery in the world, let us listen to these lines of hope by the poet C. Day Lewis:

'His laughter was better than birds in the morning, his smile
Turned the edge of the wind, his memory
Disarms death and charms the surly grave.
Early he went to bed, too early we
Saw his light put out; yet we could not grieve
More than a little while,
For he lives in the earth around us, laughs from the sky.'

SECOND CEREMONY

This ceremony was held for someone who died in old age after a long and full life.

Opening Words

We are meeting here today to honor the life of Anne Smith and to bring consolation to those of her family and friends who are here. Our ceremony will be a short and simple one, which will be in keeping with what she would have liked.

The world is a community, and Anne has been a part of that community. We are all involved in the life and death of each of us. Human life is built on caring.

Thought on Life and Death

It is natural that we should be sad today, because in a practical sense Anne is no longer a part of our lives. But we should not grieve—to live a good and fulfilling life for ninety years, with only the last year seriously marred by failing health, and then to die in one's sleep, is something to be thankful for.

I don't think there is anyone who does not feel themselves enriched by having known her. She will be remembered as a mother, a mother-in-law, a grandmother, and a friend. Her influence lives on in the unending consequences that flow from her life and character.

Boris Pasternak wrote:

'However far back you go in your memory, it is always in some external, active manifestation of yourself that you come across your identity—in the work of your hands, in your family, in other people...this is what you are. This is what your consciousness has breathed and lived on, and enjoyed throughout your life ...your immortality, your life in others. And what now? What does it matter to you if, later on, it is called your 'memory'? This will be you—the real you—that enters the future and becomes a part of it.'

All living I things are subject to death: it is the basis of growth. Through evolution, in the course of millions upon millions of deaths, humanity has evolved. We carry this inheritance. But we, as human individuals, have a more personal contribution to make, in the value of our own lives. And those of us who accept the unity and completeness of the natural order, and believe that to die means the end of the conscious personality, look death in the face with honesty, with dignity, and with calm.

Bertrand Russell wrote:

'An individual human existence should be like a river—small at first, narrowly contained within its banks, and rushing passionately past boulders and over waterfalls. Gradually the river grows wider, the banks recede, the waters flow more quietly, and—in the end—without any visible break, they become merged in the sea, and painlessly lose their individual being. The man or woman who, in old age, can see his or her life in this way, will not suffer from the fear of death, since the things they care for will continue.'

To choose a poem to read on this occasion was a near impossibility. Anne's love of literature, and poetry in particular, was profound. Even when her memory was failing she could still reel off verse upon verse of her favorite poems, in a variety of languages. A. E. Housman was a special favorite:

'Tell me not here, it needs not saying
What tune the enchantress plays
In aftermaths of soft September
Or under blanching mays,
For she and I were long acquainted
And I knew all her ways.

On russet floors, by waters idle,
The pine lets fall its cone;
The cuckoo shouts all day at nothing
In leafy dells alone;
And traveller's joy beguiles in Autumn
Hearts that have lost their own.

On acres of the seeded grasses
The changing burnish heaves;
Or marshalled under moons of harvest
Stands still all night the sheaves;
Or beeches strip in storms for Winter
And stain the wind with leaves.

Possess, as I possessed a season,
The countries I resign,
Where over elmy plains the highway
Would mount the hills and shine,
And full of shade the pillared forest
Would murmur and be mine.

For Nature, heartless, witless Nature,
Will neither care nor know
What stranger's feet may find the meadow
And trespass there and go,
Nor ask amid the dews of morning
It they are mine or no."

Tribute by One of Anne's grandsons

'Anne was the last Victorian member of our family. Her life spanned some huge changes, but Anne always adapted to those changes; the changes of customs and views of those around her she took in her stride. She might I think stand as an example to anyone, of which Victorian values are worth cherishing, and which are worth thinking about changing.

When she was a child she was the tiny one of the family, and she used to hold her own by using the back leg of her wooden horse Cossack to fend off others. I think that might be a difficult picture to imagine, but though in later life her pacifism led her away from using weapons it perhaps at least shows that she was always a formidable woman. When she was a child she had diphtheria. It was rare to survive that, but she did survive it; and I think perhaps that set the course for the rest of her life, which saw more than its fair share of terrible events—the death of her mother in childbirth, the death of her brother in the first war, the death of her husband after four years of marriage. I think the strength and stoicism involved in dealing with those events carried through every aspect of her life.

Some of that strength must have been needed in her career, in going through the law exams, in becoming one of this country's first women barristers, and in campaigning for penal reform. Her passionate involvement in issues—pacifism, the Labour party, politics in general, current affairs—had its roots in her family and in the atmosphere of high liberal thought in which she was brought up. But it stretched right through her life.

Her reading was quite extraordinary. We must all at times have been astonished by the range and depth of her knowledge, much of it from books, but also from her own experience. For me and for many of us she is an irreplaceable resource as a fountain of knowledge, whether or not what one wanted was a translation of the words of a Schubert song, or help with writing a letter to complain to someone, or research for historical plays. I can think of the amount of knowledge she had—anything you wanted to ask her she was likely to know, and relatively likely to have had some kind of personal connection with. There was no show involved in this: she would tell you anything without ever making you feel foolish for not knowing it in the first place.

Anne always loved being out of doors. She was intrepid in her walking and swimming,—even this Autumn she spent a great deal of time out in the garden whatever the weather.

In recent years not being able to go so far afield perhaps increased her already great interest in everybody else's activities. I'm sure we must all have felt the depth of interest and appreciation of everything we did: she unfailingly kept up with what everyone was doing.

The enormous influence that she has had on family and friends is perhaps most evident in ways of talking; in phrases, in ways of understating things, in a love and respect for words.

But Anne has been an example to us all not just of ways of talking but a whole approach to life, which we have each absorbed in big or little ways, directly and indirectly. She was in some ways very extreme: she was extremely generous, she was extremely reserved, but underneath a very good deal more emotional than she was willing to show. She was phenomenally self-controlled; she was a great optimist. She remembers her being optimistic about the weather, but about all things she was an optimist. She was a great wit, and she had the kind of judgement which we always trusted without question. I'm sure that each of us will remember different stories, different comments, different feelings from our contact with Anne; but she has made a huge impact on our world. And it's not difficult to see that around us and within us. To say she was a wonderful grandmother is nothing: she was a magnificent inspiration, and will continue to be so.

We may all owe different debts to Anne's wisdom, but perhaps one thought that she was fond of repeating is the right one on which to end. She always impressed on us that if ever any opportunity arose we must take it. She herself provided many of us with a great many opportunities, and this celebration of her life provides us with another.'

I will now ask you to remain silent for a moment or two, so that you call each remember Anne in your own way. (Pause of 30 seconds)

The Committal

Will you now stand for the committal.

> 'To everything there is a season, and a time to every purpose on earth...a time to be born, and a time to die.'

Here, in this last act, in sorrow but without fear, in love and appreciation, we commit Anne's body to its natural end.

Closing Words and Music

Thank you all for joining with us to celebrate Anne's full and long life. Before we go home I will say a word about the music. All the pieces we have chosen are ones that Anne particularly liked. As you came in you heard The Prisoners' Chorus from Fidelio; you are now going to hear Emma singing 'An die Musik'; and this will be followed—as we go out—by the first movement of Mozart's G Minor Symphony.

THIRD CEREMONY

> This is a ceremony for a child of 2 years. It was followed by burial.

Opening Words

Friends, we meet here today to celebrate the life of Susan Jones. (Please be seated.)

This is a sad day, especially sad because grief for the loss of a child is hardest to bear. When an old person dies we may grieve, but we can accept more readily that a life has been lived and has drawn to its inevitable close. But when a child dies, we mourn not only the life that was, but also the life that might have been. It is right, and natural that we should grieve, because sorrow is a reflection and measure of the love, the happiness and the intimacy we shared with the one who has gone. In a way too we grieve for ourselves, because we know that our own lives will never be the same without her.

Inevitably you will find the world a poorer place without Susan, but it will always be a richer place because she was once in it, so the joy of having a daughter, a granddaughter, a sister, a niece, a young friend, may indeed be lost; but the joy of having had that relationship, the delight and comfort of its memories, is never lost. There never has been and never will be anyone in the world like Susan, and she will live in your memories not just at special times like birthdays, but always. She will always remain a part of the family.

Thoughts on Life and Death

So we are here not just to mourn, but also to celebrate Susan's life. It was of course a very short short life, but I would like to suggest to you that our habit of measuring the worth or quality of a life by its duration is a bad one. Time does not bring out what matters most in life. I can best illustrate what I mean by quoting the words of two very different writers. First, the great Russian novelist Alexander Solzhenitsyn, who wrote:

> 'Some people are bound to die young. By dying young a person stays young forever in people's memory. If he burns brightly before he dies, his light shines for all time.'

And the 16th century dramatist Ben Jonson wrote:

> 'A lily of a day
> Is fairer far in May.
> Although it fall and die that night
> It was the plant and flower of light.'

It is the enduring brightness of Susan's life that I now want us to reflect upon.

The Tribute

That life began just 2 years ago, when Susan was born to Barbara and Tom, a sister for Janet, on May 16, 1986—so she really was a fair flower of May, just as in Jonson's poem. I never had the pleasure of knowing Susan, but I have had the privilege of seeing some photographs of her and of sharing some of Barbara and Tom's thoughts about her life.

Susan had Down's Syndrome. Most of us realize that there is still a widespread lack of understanding of this condition. There is a tendency for those who know no better to shun Down's Syndrome children, to react with unease or suspicion. I know that, through her sunny nature and her ability to make friends wherever she went, no one could have done more to dispel such reactions than Susan did in her 2 years. It is quite something to have been such a successful ambassadress for countless others, and at such an early age.

Tom has said to me that Susan had certainly given him and Barbara more than they had given her. I've thought a lot about that remark, having at least an inkling of the time and patience Barbara and Tom must have devoted to stimulating Susan from the earliest stage, together with all the usual demands of parenthood. Yet they feel that they received from her more than they gave. When some great person dies, a statesman, military man or artist perhaps, we know that honors and tributes will be poured on them and that their names may go down in the history books. But of how many of these could it he said, quite simply, that, like little Susan, they gave to life more than they took from it?

In talking to her parents, what came across to me time and again was Susan's sunny nature and also—something she shared with many other Down's Syndrome children—a tremendous pleasure in music. We are now going to hear a song—by 'Talking Heads'—which has special associations and happy memories, because Susan loved to bop around the living room to this in Barbara's arms. One of the lines goes: 'The world was good and she was right there with it!'—and that's as fitting a tribute to Susan as any you'll find. (Music: 'Little Creatures'—Talking Heads)

I'm sure that everyone who knew Susan will have no difficulty at all in picturing her delight at that, and I know that many other memories of her will be crowding in at this time. We shall now observe a brief silence, and what I want you to do is to select a special, happy memory of Susan as you knew her and would like going on remembering her. Any of you who have a religious faith might like to use these moments for your own private prayer. (SILENCE)

Closing Words

And so it is nearly time for us to depart from here to the cemetery and the committal. Our celebration of Susan's life is almost ended. But, before we go, let me make these important points. There may be some who did not know Susan who, because of her handicap, might feel that her death is 'just as well' or 'a blessing in disguise'. It is true that, as in the case of any child, death spared her the disillusion, frustration and pain which come with the awareness of growing up and growing old. As it was, she knew only happiness and love. But, as her father has told me, Susan certainly had intelligence and ability enough to have enriched the lives of others, had she lived longer, just as she did in the short span allotted to her. It is no blessing that we have lost her.

At the other extreme, there may be those who feel 'What a waste!' Looked at that way, all life is a waste, for we must all die. But the short span of a life does not mean that it is wasted. I take you back to the lily or the daffodil : what matters is not that they are short-lived, but what they bring to the world. In the same way, a holiday is not worthless because its days are numbered. Even the briefest holiday has a special value, and indeed we value it the more because its days are few.

So Susan's death was certainly no blessing; neither was it a waste. Her life is to be valued and cherished for what it was: she brought and gave happiness, she experienced tenderness and love; now that she is no more, let I that be enough.

Our concluding music, chosen by Barbara and Tom, is from Mali. Mali is a wretchedly poor North African country on the edge of the Sahara desert. For many parents in Mali the loss of a child is more routine than a ride in a car. Let us, as a final tribute to Susan, use her little life of uncomplicated happiness, together with this music, to remind us of other children...Down's Syndrome children; children in Mali and elsewhere in the Third World; all children with the same capacity for joy and pleasure as Susan; children who need the love and care and support from their world family that Susan received from her own family.

Before we listen to the music and then leave, I'd like to take this opportunity, on behalf of Barbara and Tom, to thank you for coming and for all the warmth and support and love you have given them these last weeks. I know you will continue to offer that support in the time to come, as they strive to readjust to everyday life. (Closing Music—'Ba Tagoma'—Sidiki Diabate)

Committal at a Nearby Cemetery

My friends, we have been remembering, with sadness yet with warm appreciation, the short life of Susan Jones. She is now beyond harm, fear and pain; and
here—in this last rite—we commit her body to the safe bosom of our Earth,
which sustains and regenerates all life. The memory of her life and personality we shall cherish with love and with gratitude. As we return to our homes,
to our work, to our lives, let us resolve to follow Susan's example by using our
lives more fully and to better purpose, with the same cheerfulness and deter-
mination that were so much a part of Susan's life. Thank you, my friends.

ON THE DAY

As has been mentioned above it is important to be scrupulously careful to arrive at the crematorium in good time. So make sure your transport arrangements are reliable and you allow for traffic problems. Although people do not dress up in black as they used to when attending funerals, nevertheless it is appropriate for the officiant to wear something formal and not too bright. Occasionally, perhaps for someone from a very unconventional circle, it may be agreed between you that casual clothes would be more appropriate, and this could certainly be done, though it would be rather unusual.

When you arrive at the crematorium you should be able to find one of the staff behind the scenes, even if a service is going on. If you are not familiar with that particular crematorium, the attendant will show you the controls. If you are providing the taped music, this is the best moment to hand over the cassettes—clearly labeled—to whoever will be operating the tape recorder. Give clear instructions, so that there will be no misunderstandings as to exactly when each piece of music should start and end. The person in charge of the tape recorder will bring the entry music to a close when people have all come in and settled down. If you are having music at, or immediately following, the committal, you should write out the few words leading up to the moment you want the music to begin, and hand this over to the attendant. The music on the tape for this stage should not last more than forty seconds. The cue for the exit music to start is when you step down from the lectern, though again it may be helpful to give the attendant the text of your final words.

If the family is providing the tapes, check that they have been delivered in advance (the day before is best, to give the chapel attendant time to check that the tape is set in exactly the right position and test it for volume). If you are having the organist there will be time for a few words and to go through the cues before the ceremony starts.

Arrange your text on the lectern and put any other possessions, such as a handbag or briefcase, out of sight, as you do not really want a clutter of objects in full view of everyone. There is usually a vestry where coats can be left and where you can wait, on your own if you wish until just before the ceremony is due to start. The funeral director will come and find you, while the coffin is being taken from the hearse and the mourners are getting out of their cars, which always takes a few minutes. This is also the usual time when the funeral director gives you an envelope containing your fee. You can then take up your position.

THE ARRIVAL OF THE MOURNERS

You have no need to concern yourself about the arrival of the mourners: this is the responsibility of the funeral director. If the service before is only just finishing they will be able to sit in the waiting room in privacy.

When the hearse and the car containing the chief mourners arrives, you may want to go out and greet them. There is no need to do this, except possibly on the occasions when you have not in fact met them before. If you choose to do this, it will then be expected that you lead the procession into the chapel. (Remember to walk slowly.) Alternatively, it is quite usual for the officiant to be standing at the lectern when the coffin is carried in—and in many ways this is the easiest course of action. It is a matter of personal preference.

The normal practice is for the entry music to start two or three minutes before the coffin arrives.

THE CEREMONY ITSELF

When the coffin has been brought in, the bearers withdraw, shutting the doors behind them. Often everyone will sit down of their own accord as the doors are closed and the music fades away. If they do not, it is easy to ask them quietly or even signify with a gesture that they should do so.

During the ceremony you will be facing your audience, and it is wise to project your voice to those at the back of the chapel. However, for the actual committal, officiants should turn in the direction of the coffin, to emphasize what they are doing and—as it were—as a mark of respect to the person who has died.

AFTERWARD

After you have spoken your final words and as the music starts to play, step down from the lectern, leaving your papers there, and go straight to the chief mourners. Greet whichever of them is appropriate, often the widow, widower, son or daughter whom you met when you paid your initial visit, and help to lead them gently from the chapel by the correct door.

What happens at this stage depends so much on circumstances and your relationship with the bereaved that it is difficult to generalize. Usually people will stand around for some time talking, admiring the flowers and reading the messages. It is perfectly appropriate for you to stay with the chief mourners if you wish to, until they start to leave, or you feel it is time for you to go. Some of the mourners will want to thank you, and the family may invite you to join them for refreshments. You must decide if this would or would not be appropriate. Sometimes a polite refusal is what they are really expecting; at other times it would be hurtful to refuse.

Before you leave the crematorium remember to retrieve your tapes and papers.

7 SUGGESTIONS FOR TEXTS AND TURNS OF PHRASE

This chapter consists of possible texts and turns of phrase, which may be helpful to start you off. Some of them will not be to your taste, but we hope that many will be found useful and appropriate. They are arranged in the five sections listed above, though it will be noted that several of the texts can equally well slot into one of the other sections. In particular there is considerable overlap between Sections A and B. You may wish to take passages or a few words from different texts and combine them. For example, the last words of A1 make them suitable only for an untimely death, but the rest of the text can be used more widely.

A. OPENING WORDS

1) We meet here today to celebrate/honor/pay tribute to the life of...and to express our love and admiration for h../ and to bring some consolation/comfort to those of h..family and friends who are here, and who have been hurt by h..untimely death

2) Death is a very personal matter to those who experience the death of someone close to them, but we are all concerned. I am here to represent the concern of other people—those who knew h..well, knew h..a little, or who did not know h.., but have been touched indirectly by h..life.

The world is a community and...has been a part of that community. We are all involved in the life and death of each of us. Human life is built on caring. This is the heart of Humanism. *Humanist*

3) We are all concerned, directly or indirectly, with the death of any individual, for we are all members of one human community. Though some of the links between us are strong and some are tenuous, each of us is joined to all the others by links of kinship, love or friendship; by living in the same neighborhood or town or country; or simply by our common humanity.

4) A Humanist funeral ceremony is an opportunity to join in taking leave of someone we have loved/someone for whom we have had the greatest affection/respect...but it is more than that. It is the celebration of the life and personality that have been...in this case a full and long life and a greatly loved personality.

5) The catastrophe of death cannot be altered, but it can be transformed by love. *Tragic circumstances*

6) Death comes to us all—...chose to grasp death/went to meet death.

Suicide

7) We meet to remember...and to help each other accept h.. death. S/he had grown only a little way towards human personality, but s/he was an important person in the eyes off hose who loved h.. The wider circle of h.. family and their friends care deeply about h.., death and about the grief of those close to h.., even if they find it hard to express their concern. *Infant*

8) Our ceremony will be a short and simple one, which is what...particularly wanted/would have liked. It will not be religious because that would be out of keeping with what s/he believed.

9) I want to welcome everyone who has come today. I hope that at the end of this farewell ceremony for...you will feel glad that you took the opportunity to do some of your grieving in the presence of others who have known and loved h..

10) I am here as a representative of the human community of which s/he was part.

11) As...had no religious beliefs, his family have thought it appropriate to have a non-religious ceremony. I am therefore officiating today at their request as a Humanist.

B. Thoughts on Life and Death

1) The death of each of us is in the order of things: it follows life as surely as night follows day. We can take the Tree of Life as a symbol. The human race is the trunk and branches of this tree, and individual men and women are the leaves, which appear one season, flourish for a summer, and then die. I too am like a leaf of this tree, and one day I shall be torn off by a storm, or simply decay and fall—and mingle with the earth at its roots. But, while I live, I am conscious of the tree's flowing sap and steadfast strength. Deep down in my consciousness is the consciousness of a collective life, a life of which I am a part, and to which I make a minute but unique contribution. When I die and fall the tree remains, nourished to some small degree by my manifestation of life. Millions of leaves have preceded me and millions will follow me: but the tree itself grows and endures. *Adapted from Herbert Read*

2) All living things are subject to death: it is the basis of growth. Through evolution, in the course of millions upon millions of deaths, humanity has evolved. We carry this inheritance. But we, as human individuals, have a more personal contribution to make, each in the value of our own lives.

3) The separateness, the uniqueness of each human life is the basis of our grief in bereavement. Look through the whole world and there is no one like the one you have lost. But s/he still lives on in your memories and, though no longer a visible part of your lives, s/he will always remain a member of your family or of your circle, through the influence s/he has had on you and the special part s/he has played in your lives.

4) We know that the value and the meaning of life consist in living it—and living it well. People who have been a strength and comfort to others and have

worked for future generations, deriving fulfillment and satisfaction from so doing, these are the people who bring value and meaning to life. And...was such a person.

5) All that has life has its beginning and its end. Life exists in the little span between birth and death and, for those of us who believe that death brings the end of individual existence, life's significance lies in the experiences and satisfactions we achieve in that span of time. *Humanist*

6) The comfort of having a friend—a brother, a father, a colleague*—may indeed be lost, but the comfort of having had that friend is never lost. To match the grief of losing h.., you have the joy of having known h.. —a joy of which you become especially aware at this moment, as you fix h.. living image in your minds and recall the personal qualities that made h.. unique. (*make sure you get these relationships correct!)

7) Looking beyond our grief today, we rejoice that...was, and is, a part of our lives. H.. influence endures in the unending consequences that flow from h.. character and the things s/he did. We shall remember h.. as a living, vital presence. That memory will bring refreshment to our hearts in times of trouble.

8) Those of us who accept the unity of the natural order, and believe that to die means the end of the conscious personality, look death in the face with honesty, with dignity and with calm. *Humanist*

9) For those of us who believe that death brings the end of individual existence, recognition of our responsibility for, and dependence on, each other gives life a purpose and significance. The concept of an individual life as an event in a natural cycle answers our search for a pattern of which we are part. And in our personal achievements and in the minds of those who have known us, and in our children, rests the continuance of something of ourselves.
Humanist

10) I don't think there is anyone here who does not feel enriched for having known h.. S/he will be remembered as mother*, a mother-in-law, a grandmother, a great-grandmother and a friend. (*again, be sure to get the relationships right)

11) It is natural that we should be sad today because, in a practical sense,... is no longer a part of our lives. But we should not grieve—to live a fulfilling life to a great age and then to die in one's sleep, is something to be thankful for.

12) Though it is natural for us to grieve that... and... (the deceased and the spouse) will not now enjoy the satisfaction of growing old together, let us think today about the happy years and the good times.

13) Death is as natural as life—and it is inevitable. For... it has come suddenly and by a chance accident. But chance is natural to life. The end of each of us will be determined by chance—the failure of some organ of our body, or some accidental intervention of all external cause. The mis-chance that struck... was at the limit of likelihood, but it was in the course of natural processes. We should not seek to explain chance: it is a come-together of events of no meaning.   *Accidental death*

14) Humanism has deep roots in the history of humankind: it has grown over the centuries from our search for honesty and truth, and from our love and concern for our fellow men and women.   *Humanist*

15) I now ask you to remain silent for a moment or two so that you can each think your own thoughts/you can each remember... in your own way. Those of you with religious faith may like to use these moments for your own private prayer.

16) We tend to overrate our public figures and forget those who make life worth living. The men and women whose names are writ large in history are few. We should remember those whose quality of life, though unspectacular, is built into the fabric of our civilization.   *A good link between B and C*

C. THE TRIBUTE

1) A Humanist funeral is more than a leave-taking. It is the celebration of a life that has ended.

2) H.. family and friends will remember h.. each in their own way.

3) S/he would have been proud to know how courageously and cheerfully the family are supporting each other at this difficult time.

4) Though s/he had h.. share of difficulties and of grief, s/he faced whatever came with courage/patience/good humor/stoicism.

5) S/he never felt sorry for h.. self, nor complained about h.. own troubles/illness/disability/loneliness/suffering.

6) We are glad for h.. sake that she was spared the suffering and demoralization of a long illness, and that death came to h.. so quickly and easily.

7) We think of h.. in many ways and in many situations. But most of all we picture h.. at home in h.. wonderful garden, among the vegetables s/he worked so hard to cultivate.

8) It is clear that h.. was a very special person.

9) Let us remember h.. as the fine-looking, healthy human being that s/he always was.

10) We remember ... with deep affection.

11) We remember ... as a gentle and good person, towards whom others would naturally turn for help and comfort.

12) The way we respond to the prospect of death is an expression of our own being. The way ... died was characteristic of the kind of person s/he was. S/he faced death without fear, and made it a fitting end to h.. long, full and fruitful life.

D. THE COMMITTAL

1) Let us now stand for the committal.

2) We now come to the final act in our formal parting: please stand.

3) We have reached the part in today's ceremony when ...'s body will be taken from our view. Would you please stand.

4) In love and respect we have remembered the life of ... and recalled the person s/he has been.

5) Here, in this last act, immune now to the changes and chances of our mortal lot, we commit the body of ... (full name) to its natural end.

6) H.. body we commit to it's natural end, its transformation into the ultimate elements of the universe expedited by the age-old process of fire—a primal cosmic force.

7) 'To everything there is a season, and a time to every purpose on Earth; a time to be born and a time to die ...'

8) And so death has come to our friend and loved one ... H.. hopes and ideals we commit into our minds and our wills; h.. loves we commit into our hearts; h.. spirit has long been abroad in the world. We commit h.. body to its natural end.

9) Here, in this last act, in sorrow but without fear, in love and appreciation, we commit ...'s body to its natural end.

10) And now we have come to the end of our brief ceremony and must say goodbye to the body of ... S/he will be remembered as a ...

E. CLOSING WORDS

1) We have been remembering with love and with gratitude a life that has ended. Let its now return to our homes and to our work, resolved that we who live on will use our lives more fully and to better purpose for having known ... and for having shared in h.. life.

2) The best of all answers to death is the whole-hearted and continuing affirmation of life, for the greater fulfillment of humankind.

3) Friends, we have been remembering with love and humility/appreciation/affection/ a life now ended. Now we must each return to living our own lives, enriched by these memories, so that those who live may have life more fully.

4) In respect and appreciation we remember the long life of... and its fullness of experience.

5) In sadness for h.. death but in gratitude for h.. life, we remember... and h.. talent for joy and love.

6) In love we shall keep the memory of... and in gratitude we recall the human image s/he has left us. And now we have each other. That is all we have, but it is all we need. We are subject to natural law and to chance, but our humanity gives us the power to stand over and against them. We have a measure of understanding and so we gain some control. We share our thoughts and our feelings, and so support each other. By our living and our loving we create the values of the world.

7) I hope you have derived some comfort from gathering here today.

8) In a little while we will he going out into the world renewed and heartened. Some of you will be returning to your homes or to work. Find friends and support each other. Remember how you felt sharing your thoughts and feelings; how much more bearable your pain is when it is shared.

9) On behalf of... and... (spouse next of kin close friend) I like to thank you for joining with us to celebrate ...'s life and personality, and for all the support and sympathy that you have given over the last days, weeks/months.

10) To send us on our way let us sit for a few minutes and listen to...

8 POETRY AND PROSE READINGS

You will find on the following pages a brief selection of poems and a few prose passages. People who officiate at funerals on a regular basis usually have their own collections of favorite readings, but these take some time to build up. Our suggestions may save a firsttimer some hours of frantic burrowing through anthologies. The poems reproduced here are some that encapsulate thoughts and feelings you may be seeking to put across. They are arranged as far as possible in different sections. Titles of helpful anthologies are given in the book list at the back of this booklet.

There are a number of suitable poems by living poets which have not been included for reasons of copyright, but they are certainly worth looking for. Also it is sometimes nice to include poems or prose passages that were known to be much loved by the person who has died (see the second ceremony). In that case of course the poems may be on any subject, they are often chosen by the family or friends, and we are not dealing with these personal choices here.

Some officiants are not particularly keen on reciting poetry, and in this case, if a poem is wanted, it is possible to play a tape read by a professional actor. Or sometimes a relative or friend will read a prose passage or poem that they have chosen, or make a recording themselves.

DO NOT GRIEVE

Song

When I am dead, my dearest,
Sing no sad songs for me;
Plant thou no roses at my head,
Nor shady cypress tree:
Be the green grass above me
With showers and dewdrops wet;
And if thou wilt, remember,
And if thou wilt, forget.

I shall not see the shadows,
I shall not feel the rain;
I shall not hear the nightingale
Sing on, as if in pain;
And dreaming through the twilight
That doth not rise nor set,
Haply I may remember,
And haply may forget.

Christina Rossetti

Remember

Remember me when I am gone away,
Gone far away into the silent land;
When you can no more hold me by the hand,
Nor I half turn to go yet turning stay.
Remember me when no more day by day
You tell me of our future that you planned:
Only remember me; you understand
It will be late to counsel then or pray.
Yet if you should forget me for a while
And afterwards remember, do not grieve:
For if the darkness and corruption leave
A vestige of the thoughts that once I had,
Better by far you should forget and smile
Than that you should remember and be sad.

Christina Rossetti

Requiem

Under the wide and starry sky,
Dig the grave and let me lie.
Glad did I live and gladly die,
And I laid me down with a will.

This be the verse you grave for me:
Here he lies where he longed to be;
Home is the sailor, home from sea,
And the hunter home from the hill.

R. L. Stevenson

If it must be
You speak no more with us,
Nor smile no more with us,
Nor walk no more with us,
Then let us take a patience and a calm.
For even now the green leaf explodes,
Sun lightens stone, and all the river burns.

Anon, from Central America

If I Should Die

If I should die and leave you
Be not like others, quick undone
Who keep long vigil by the silent
dust and weep.

For my sake turn to life and smile
Nerving thy heart and trembling
hand to comfort weaker souls
        than thee.
Complete these unfinished tasks
        of mine
And I perchance may therein
        comfort thee.

Thomas Gray

THE PEACE OF DEATH

"For thou shalt sleep and never wake again,
And, quitting life, shall quit all living pain;
But we, they friends, shall all those sorrows find
Which in forgetful death thou leav'st behind."

Lucretius (trans. Dryden)

A late lark twitters from the quiet skies;
And from the west,
Where the sun, his days work ended,
Lingers as in content
There falls on the old, gray city
An influence luminous and serene,
A shining peace.
The smoke ascends
In a rosy-and-golden haze. The spires
Shine, and are changed. In the valley
Shadows rise. The lark sings on. The sun,
Closing his benediction
Sinks, and the darkening air
Thrills with a sense of the triumphing night—
Night with her train of stars
And her great gift of sleep

So be my passing!
My task accomplished and the long day done,
My wages taken, and in my heart
Some late lark singing,
Let me be gathered to the quiet west,
The sundown splendid and serene, Death.

W. E. Henley

From too much love of living,
From hope and fear set free,
We thank with brief thanksgiving
Whatever gods may be
That no life lives for ever;
That dead men rise up never;
That even the weariest river
Winds somewhere safe to sea.

Then star nor sun shall waken,
Nor any change of light:
Nor sound of waters shaken,
Nor any sound or sight:
Nor wintry leaves nor vernal,
Nor days nor things diurnal;
Only the sleep eternal
In an eternal night.

Swinburne

Goodnight; ensured release,
Imperishable peace,
Have these for yours,
While sea abides, and land,
And earth's foundations stand,
And heaven endures.
When earth's foundations flee,
Nor sky nor land nor sea
At all is found,
Content you, let them burn:
It is not your concern;
Sleep on, sleep sound.

A. E. Housman

FOR THOSE WHO DIE YOUNG

"Doomed to know not Winter; only Spring—a being
Trod the flowery April blithely for a while;
Took his fill of music, joy of though and seeing,
Came and stayed and went; nor ever ceased to smile.

Came and stayed and went; and now, when all is finished,
You alone have crossed the melancholy stream.
Yours the pang; but his, oh his, the undiminished
Undecaying gladness, undeparted dream."

R. L. Stevenson

He has outsoared the shadow of our night;
Envy and calumny and hate and pain,
And that unrest which men miscall delight,
Can touch him not and torture not again;
From the contagion of the world's slow stain
He is secure, and now can never mourn
A heart grown cold, a head grown gray in vain;

He is made one with Nature; there is heard
His voice in all her music, from the moan
Of thunder, to the song of night's sweet bird;
He is a presence to be felt and known
In darkness and in light…

He is a portion of the loveliness
Which once he made more lovely…

P. B. Shelley

Fear no more the heat o' the sun,
Nor the furious winter's rages;
Thou thy worldly task hast done,
Home art gone, and ta'en they wages.
Golden lads and girls all must,
As chimney-sweepers, come to dust.

Fear no more the frown o' the great,
Thou art past the tyrant's stroke;
Care no more to clothe and eat,
To thee the reed is as the oak
The sceptre, learning, physic, must
All follow this, and come to dust.

Fear no more the lightning-flash,
Nor the all-dreaded thunder-stone;
Fear not slander, censure rash;
Thou has finished joy and moan.
All lovers young, all lovers must
Consign to thee, and come to dust.

William Shakespeare

Fair daffodils, we weep to see
You haste away so soon;
As yet the early-rising sun
Has not attained his noon.
Stay, stay
Until the hasting day
Has run
But to the evensong;
And, having prayed together, we
Will go with you along.

We have short time to stay as you,
We have as short a spring;
As quick a growth to meet decay
As you, or anything.
We die
As your hours do, and dry
Away
Like to the summer's rain;
Or as the pearls of morning's dew,
Ne'er to be found again.

Robert Herrick

THE NATURAL ORDER

I was not. I have been. I am not. I do not mind. *(Epicurean epitaph)*

Become accustomed to the belief that death is nothing to us. For all good and evil consists in sensation, but death is deprivation of sensation. And therefore a right understanding that death is nothing to us makes the mortality of life enjoyable, not because it adds to it an infinite span of time, but because it takes away the craving for immortality. For there is nothing terrible in life for the man who has truly comprehended that there is nothing terrible in not living.

Epicurus

Like as the waves make towards the pebbled shore,
So do our minutes hasten to their end;
Each changing place with that which goes before,
In sequent toil all forwards do contend.
Nativity, once in the main of light,
Crawls to maturity, wherewith being crowned,
Crooked eclipses 'gainst his glory fight,
And Time that gave doth now his gift confound.
Time doth transfix the flourish set on youth
And delves the parallels in beauty's brow,
Feeds on the rarities of nature's truth,
And nothing stands but for his scythe to mow.
And yet to times in hope my verse shall stand,
Praising thy worth, despite his cruel hand.

William Shakespeare

No single thing abides; but all things flow.
Fragment to fragment clings—the things thus grow
Until we know and name them. By degrees
They melt, and are no more the things we know.

Globed from the atoms falling slow or swift
I see the suns, I see the systems lift
Their forms; and even the systems and the suns
Shall go back slowly to the eternal drift.

Thou too, oh earth—thine empires, lands, and seas—
Least, with thy stars, of all the galaxies,
Globed from the drift like these, like these thou too
Shalt go. Thou art going, hour by hour, like these.

Nothing abides. Thy seas in delicate haze
Go off; those mooned sands forsake their place;
And where they are, shall other seas in turn
Mow with their scythes of whiteness other bays...

The seeds that once were we take flight and fly,
Winnowed to earth, or whirled along the sky,
Not lost but disunited. Life lives on.
It is the lives, the lives, the lives, that die.

Lucretius

Cities and Thrones and Powers
Stand in Time's eye,
Almost as long as flowers,
Which daily die:
But, as new buds put forth
To glad new men,
Out of the spent and
      unconsidered Earth
The Cities rise again.

This season's Daffodil
She never hears
What change, what chance,
      what chill,
Cut down last year's;
But with bold countenance,
And knowledge small,
Esteems her seven days'
      continuance
To be perpetual.

So Time that is oer kind
To all that be,
Ordains us e'en as blind,
As bold as she:
That in our very death,
And burial sure,
Shadow to shadow,
      well persuaded, saith,
'See how our works endure!'

Rudyard Kipling

LIVING ON IN PEOPLE'S MEMORIES

I fall asleep in the full and certain hope
That my slumber shall not be broken;
And that though I be all-forgetting,
Yet shall I not be all-forgotten,
But continue that life in the
    thoughts and deeds
Of those I loved…

Samuel Butler

They told me. Heraclitus, they told me
    you were dead,
They brought me bitter news to hear and
    bitter tears to shed.
I wept as I remember how often you and I
Had tired the sun with talking and sent him
    down the sky.

And now that thou art lying, my dear old
    Carian guest,
A handful of grey ashes, long, long ago at rest,
Still are they pleasant voices, they nightingales,
    awake;
For Death, he taketh all away,
    but them he cannot take.

W. J. Cory

When the Present has latched its postern behind my tremulous stay,
And the May month flaps its glad green leaves like wings,
Delicate-filmed as new-spun silk, will the neighbours say,
'He was a man who used to notice such things'?

If it be in the dusk when, like an eyelids soundless blink,
The dewfall-hawk comes crossing the shades to alight
Upon the wind-warped upland thorn, a gazer may think,
'To him this must have been a familiar sight.'

If I pass during some nocturnal blackness, mothy and warm,
When the hedgehog travels furtively over the lawn,
One may say, 'He strove that such innocent creatures should come to no harm,
But he could do little for them; and now he is gone.'

If, when hearing that I have been stilled at last, they stand at the door,
Watching the full-starred heavens that winter sees,
Will this thought rise on those who will meet my face no more,
'He was one who had an eye for such mysteries'?

And will any say when my bell of quittance is heard in the gloom,
And a crossing breeze cuts a pause in its outrollings,
Till they rise again, as they were a new bell's boom,
'He hears it not now, but used to notice such things'?

Thomas Hardy

O may I join the choir invisible
Of those immortal dead who live again
In minds made better by their presence: live
In pulses stirred to generosity,
In deeds of daring rectitude, in scorn
For miserable aims that end with self,
In thoughts sublime that pierce the night like stars,
And with their mild persistence urge man's search
To vaster issues...
This is the life to come,
Which martyred men have made more glorious
For us who strive to follow. May I reach
That purest heaven, be to other souls
The cup of strength in some great agony,
Enkindle generous ardour, feed pure love,
Beget the smiles that have no cruelty—
Be the sweet presence of a good diffused,
And in diffusion ever more intense.
So shall I join the choir invisible
Whose music is the gladness of the world.

George Eliot

HEREDITY

I am the family face;
Flesh perishes, I live on,
Projecting trait and trace
Through time to times anon,
And leaping from place to place
Over oblivion.

The years-heired feature that can
In curve and voice and eye
Despise the human span
Of durance—that is I;
The eternal thing in man,
That heeds no call to die.

Thomas Hardy

Music, when soft voices die,
Vibrates in the memory;
Odours, when sweet violets sicken,
Live within the sense they quicken.

Rose leaves, when the rose is dead,
Are heaped for the beloved's bed;
And so thy thoughts, when thou art gone,
Love itself shall slumber on.

P. B. Shelley

SUICIDE

If I can choose between a death of torture and one that is simple and easy, why should I not select the latter? As I choose the ship in which I sail and the house which I inhabit, so will I choose the death by which I leave life.

Seneca

MUSIC

The choice of music for a funeral ceremony is very important and it should ideally be made by the family or friends, bearing in mind what the dead person would have liked (or in some cases had actually requested). However, if no special interest in the choice of music is shown by the family, then it is for you to make suitable suggestions and give advice. It is as well to point out to them that some people try to avoid choosing music of which they are particularly fond, as they do not wish to have it permanently associated with grief in their minds.

When choosing the music it will first be necessary to decide whether to make use of the organist, who is almost invariably available, or to make use of the cassette player that most crematoria now provide. (It is worth noting that in some crematoria the organist comes free of charge while use of the cassette player is charged for, and in some places it is the other way round. The funeral director should give this information to the family). A third option is to have a live performance. As has been mentioned elsewhere, this is especially suitable when someone in the musical world has died. But, as it is relatively uncommon and as the music will be chosen by the participants, it is inappropriate to go into details here.

USING THE ORGANIST

From the point of view of the officiant, the easiest option is to use the services of the organist. Once you have found out what there is in the way of secular music, and the pieces have been chosen, that is the end of your responsibility in the matter. All that remains is for you to give details of timing and actual cues to the organist just before the ceremony.

However there are two possible difficulties: first, the organist's repertoire of secular music may not include the piece that is wanted; and second, for some people, the sound of organ music is inextricably associated in their minds with church services. The second point is perhaps a minor problem to be overcome, but the first point—the prospect of not being able to choose the music that is wanted—may prove to be a considerable drawback. You may be able to prevail on the organist to learn a piece of music not normally in the repertoire—and some organists positively welcome a new idea—but this is only reasonable if there is some time in hand.

USING TAPED MUSIC

Most crematoria now have facilities for playing tapes. Where this is the case, and if there is a shortage of appropriate music, officiants can all too easily find themselves saddled with the job of providing the taped music. As with the readings, someone who officiates regularly can soon build up a supply of suitable tapes, which will ease the burden of making last minute recordings. But it can be troublesome, particularly if you have no recording facilities yourself. We recommend that you tell the family what tapes are available and ask them to select something, or else to allow you to choose some suitable pieces. If they want something that is not available, it is reasonable to suggest that they organize this themselves, and deliver the tapes to the crematorium the day before the funeral. Sometimes, if they have the facilities, a member of the family or a friend will undertake to prepare the recordings. But whoever does it is well advised to carry out the following procedures scrupulously, as this will make the risk of technical hitches less likely:

- check that there are play-back facilities at the crematorium;
- use separate good quality tapes, each of which has been wiped clean of anything else (on both sides!);
- record on side A only, and label the tapes clearly ENTRY, COMMITTAL (if you are having music then) and EXIT;
- run each tape to the place where the music will start immediately it is switched on to play, as even a short lead-up can feel like an eternity;

CHOICE OF MUSIC

There is nothing to restrict the kind of music that can be played at funeral ceremonies: it is all a matter of personal taste. However, the length of each piece is of some importance. Normally one will want about six to eight minutes of entry music, as this may start well before the ceremony begins; a few bars only for the committal (if there is to be any music then); and five minutes or so of exit music.

People vary considerably about how solemn they feel the music should be. There is a tendency to want a fairly solemn piece at the beginning, to set the tone of the occasion, and a somewhat brisker and more cheerful piece at the end, to raise people's spirits as they leave. Some very slow and somber bars are usually chosen for the committal. There is a wealth of music to choose from, and all we do here is to make a few suggestions, covering a wide range of mood.

SOME SUGGESTIONS

If something very mournful is wanted there are the well known and moving funeral marches by Chopin (from the B flat minor Sonata, opus 35), Handel (the Dead March from 'Saul') or Beethoven (from the A flat Sonata, opus 26). Other pieces in the same vein could be Dido's Lament from Purcell's 'Dido and Aeneas', Ravel's Pavane for a Dead Princess, or Chopin's F minor Nocturne, opus 55 no 1. Examples of slow and rather solemn but less mournful music might be Handel's Largo, Nimrod from Elgar's Enigma Variations, or Samuel Barber's Adagio for Strings.

Often there is a desire for less doleful music. Beethoven's 'Ode to Joy' from his Ninth Symphony, or one of the well known marches, such as the RAF March or the Dambusters' March, or the theme music from *Chariots of Fire*, are all cheerful tunes, particularly suitable for going out.

The most common situation is that the family will expect classical music, but of course there are many other possibilities. Where the person who has died had connections with other musical traditions, the music could well reflect this. Jazz, Pop, Rock, Country and Western, Reggae, or Indian music, for example, would all be perfectly appropriate in the right context.

There have been several well publicized cases recently of funerals where unexpectedly lively music was played—the theme song from *Cabaret*, 'There's No Business Like Show Business', and 'In the Mood'. It is interesting to note that, in each of these cases, the music was chosen by the person who died. These were certainly unconventional choices, but they illustrate the very wide variation in what people feel to be appropriate. There is much to be said for well known tunes, which can be especially comforting. The Londonderry Air or Greensleeves are often played, though when songs are chosen care must be taken to see that the words are apt.

Committal Music

As has been said before, some officiants prefer not to have any music at all at the moment of committal. They feel that it interferes with the intensity of emotion when the coffin disappears from view. Others find that the music takes away some of the harshness of the moment and makes it more bearable. Once again this is a matter of taste, and it is for the individual officiant to make the choice, with the next of kin.

As the timing is so delicate, the importance of having the tape in the right position can scarcely be overstated. The tone of the committal music is usually solemn or poignant. The last few bars of Chopin's Prelude in C minor are an example of something that can suitably be played.

10 COPING WITH BEREAVEMENT

It is now widely recognized that counselling can play a crucial part in helping people to recover from the effects of a bereavement. One of the good outcomes of the major disasters that have happened in this country and elsewhere over recent years has been that the public has been made aware, through documentary television programs and newspaper articles, of the extent to which bereavement counselling can help. Much has now been written on the subject, and some of this material is of general interest to anyone coming into contact with the bereaved, perhaps for the first time.

We are not suggesting here that someone conducting a funeral ceremony will inevitably have to involve themselves in such counseling. However, it is helpful to be aware of the kind of feelings that the bereaved family and friends may be experiencing at the time you meet them, to learn about the various stages of grief, and even to know of ways in which you can give them help and support. Suggestions for reading on the subject are given in the booklist at the back of this booklet.

Loneliness, particularly for someone who has lost their partner, is something you might be able to help over in a small way, particularly if you have a local Humanist group in your area. People are often too afraid to intrude on a person's grief, when friendship and neighborliness might be a real help. A local group may well have other members in a similar situation, who would have much to share with the newly bereaved. Humanist organizations in a number of other European countries and in the United States have sophisticated counseling services.

11 SPECIAL CASES

From time to time a regular officiant, will be asked to conduct a funeral ceremony which presents particular problems, and there are some important points that need to be borne in mind. The most common of these categories are listed below:

Suicides

Some aspects of a ceremony for someone who has committed suicide will differ very little from the ceremony for someone who has perhaps died in an accident. However, it is necessary to be scrupulously careful in the words you use, and a lot will depend on the feelings of the family. There are occasions when they ask that one should avoid any reference to the fact that it was a suicide, as there may be people present who are unaware of this. In that event one must respect their wishes and treat the case as one would any sudden death.

If the family want you to refer to the nature of the death, then you should do so briefly in the course of the ceremony, in a quite open way. Try to be positive about it. In the case of a terminally ill or old person who has chosen to bring their own suffering to an end, it would he appropriate to refer to their great courage and unselfishness, and the moral rightness of what they did. When, as is too often the case, the death has been of a young person in the prime of life, then it is harder to find things to say (see chapter 7 for suggested texts). You could stress the sensitivity of the young person, which made it impossible to cope with living in today's world, and emphasize all the worthwhile things he or she managed to achieve in such a short span.

If it is possible to do so, make a point of mentioning the love and support of the family and friends, as they will inevitably be suffering a heavy load of guilt that they did not manage to prevent the suicide.

Children

Funeral ceremonies for babies and young children are perhaps the hardest to conduct. For these, more than for any others, the wishes of the family —in this case probably the parents—must be paramount. When the baby has died at birth or during the first few days or weeks of life, it will he impossible to find things to say about its life. The ceremony will undoubtedly be a very sad and emotional occasion, and will have to consist of some simple poems and music, and must focus on the parents and their shared grief and love for the child that might have been (see chapters 7 and 8 for suitable texts and poems). The ceremony itself will help them to accept that they have lost the baby. When the baby was somewhat older—even only a few months old—it will have started to develop a definite personality, which can now he remembered and celebrated. The child, even in its short life, will have given and received much love, and a lot can be made of this in the ceremony.

It is important to bear in mind, when the child who has died was suffering from grave disability, that the parents may well be agonisingly torn between their love for the child, their relief that all is over—for the child's sake and for their own—and deep feelings of guilt. Such cases require extremely sensitive handling. One response is very well brought out in our third sample ceremony, which also contains some good sections on the perfect nature of a child's life.

Those Who Are Alone

Sadly there are a great many old people who die, often in geriatric hospitals or wards, having outlived or lost touch with all close relatives and friends. If the old person has been in care for many years, perhaps confused and unable to communicate, there is sometimes no one who knows much about their earlier life, or what they were like when they were younger. There are other people who, by choice or circumstance, have led solitary lives and cut themselves off from society. With little or no information about such people's background, the officiant has no option but to compose a ceremony which largely consists of generalizations about life and death and the natural order of things, and play some music. The same unfortunately must apply when the family can find nothing positive to contribute about their elderly relative's life and personality.

OTHER FORMS OF CEREMONY

Burials

Burials are comparatively rare among Humanists, but occasionally we are asked to conduct a ceremony, followed by burial at a municipal cemetery. In this event the procedure is usually exactly the same up to the point of committal. When a burial is to follow, the officiant will be required to lead any mourners who wish to the graveside. We recommend that you have either a few flowers or a little earth available by you, so that, as you say your words of committal, you can scatter these onto the coffin. After your closing words, the mourners will disperse.

Memorial Meetings

A cremation, attended only by the immediate family, followed a few weeks or even months later by a memorial meeting, is quite often chosen when someone distinguished has died. In this event you may be asked to conduct an extremely short and basic ceremony for the family at the crematorium. There is clearly no need at all for all elaborate tribute at the cremation, merely something dignified and brief, a few general comments and some music. Less commonly you may be asked to help at the memorial meeting too, where there will be arranged speeches, readings and music, and sometimes the opportunity for impromptu tributes and anecdotes from friends and colleagues.

Other Arrangements

When the body is not there, either because it was left to medical research or following some accident or disaster, the ceremony will inevitably take the form of a memorial meeting, with no committal. When the family are anxious to organize a ceremony to bury or scatter ashes, this can involve a brief tribute and some appropriate words.

Suggestions for Further Reading

On Death and Bereavement

Memorials—an Anthology of Poetry and Prose, ed. June Benn (Ravette, 1986)
D. J. Enright, *The Oxford Book of Death* (Oxford University Press, 1983)
What to Do When Someone Dies (Consumers' Association, 1986)
Corliss Lamont, *Man Answers Death* (Watts, 1952)
Colin Murray Parkes, *Bereavement: Studies of Grief in Adult Life* (Pelican Books, 1975)
Elizabeth Collick, *Through Grief—The Bereavement Journey* (Darton, Longman and Todd)

On Humanism

Corliss Lamont, *The Philosophy of Humanism* (pub. USA, available Rationalist Press Association)
Barbara Smoker, *Humanism* (Ward Lock 1973; National Secular Society 1984)
Paul Kurtz, *Forbidden Fruit: The Ethics of Humanism* (Prometheus Books, 1988)

(Leaflets on Humanism will be sent free of charge by the British Humanist Association, 13, Prince of Wales Terrace, London W8 5PG. Advice on obtaining the books by Corliss Lamont may be sought from the Rationalist Press Association, 88, Islington High St. London N1.)

This booklet has been written and compiled by Jane Wynne Willson for the British Humanist Association. She acknowledges with gratitude the help of the following, who contributed encouragement, material, ideas and constructive criticism: Bill Brown, Maeve Denby, Sue Lines, C. D. Miller, Joan Knowles, George Mepham, Brian Nicol, Richard Paterson, Diana Rookledge,

Allan Shell, Barbara Smoker, Harry Stopes-Roe, Nicolas Walter, Robin Wood, and members of her own family.

She thanks the executors of the estate of C. Day Lewis and also Jonathan Cape and the Hogarth Press for permission to reprint 'A Time to Dance'; and Richard Scott Simon Ltd. for permission to include the poem by Joyce Grenfell.